Welcome to the world
of Foundation cursive handwriting!
Here you'll meet sea creatures,
monsters and pirates.
You might even find
some buried treasure!
This page is your passport –
so before you go any further,
fill in the information below.
Name:
Class:
Age:
Birthday:
Favourite food:
Favourite place:
Favourite activity:
Draw yourself here.
AF585547

You have been shipwrecked on a treasure island. Trace each letter or join when you have learned it, and follow the steps to the buried treasure.
Start Here
d
v
j
n
on
af
wi
ra

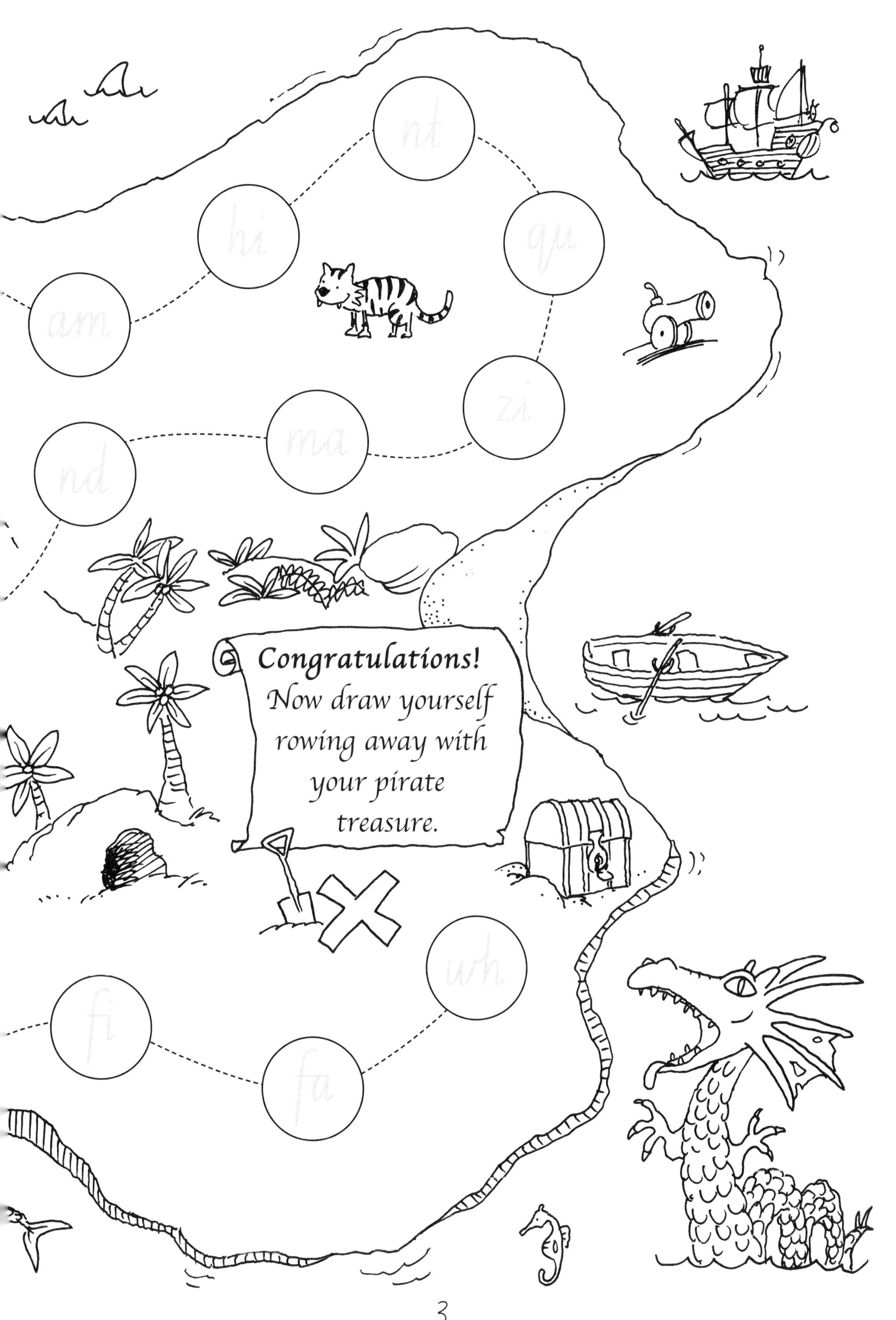
nt
hi
qu
am
zi
ma
nd
Congratulations!
Now draw yourself
rowing away with
your pirate
treasure.
wh
fi
fa

Revision – Foundation printing

Trace these capitals. Write the matching lower-case letters.

A B C D E F

G H I J K L

M N O P Q

R S T U V

W X Y Z

Trace the downstroke pattern letters in one colour. Trace the clockwise (hopping) pattern letters in another colour. Trace the anti-clockwise (wave) pattern letters in a third colour.

a b c d e f g h i

j k l m n o p q r

s t u v w x y z

Trace and copy.

1 1 1 2 2 2

3 3 3 4 4 4

5 5 5 6 6 6

7 7 7 8 8 8

9 9 9 10 10

. . . , , , ! ! !

: : : ; ; ; ' ' '

? ? ? " " " "

Revision – Letter size and position

Look at the song below. Some of the letters are the wrong size, and some are in the wrong position. Rewrite it correctly.

A sailor went to Sea, sea, sea
TO see what he Could see, see, see
ANd all that he could see, See, see
Was the bottom of the deeP blue
sea, Sea, sea!

Revision – Downstroke pattern letters

Trace. Copy. Write the matching capital letter.

Write some words you know that use only downstroke letters. You can use the same letter more than once. The first one has been done for you.

fit

Mark the starting point on these letters in green. Trace them. Draw a seahorse next to each one. Colour it to show where the letter sits in the lines.

Revision – Clockwise movement letters

Find the clockwise movement letters in these patterns.

Trace. Colour the wedges. Copy.

h p b r

n m k

Write each clockwise movement letter in the correct column. Write its capital next to it.

head and body letters	body only letters	body and tail letters

Mark the starting point in orange. Trace, then copy.

m n r h

b p k

Revision – Anti-clockwise movement letters

Trace. Circle the anti-clockwise movement letters.

a b c d e f g

h i j k l m n

o p q r s t u

v w x y z

Write the capitals that match the anti-clockwise movement letters.

Write the anti-clockwise movement letters that have a body only.

Write the anti-clockwise movement letters that have a body and tail.

Mark the starting point in purple. Trace, then copy.

q w g o

u y a c

e d v s

Introducing exits

Letters that finish at a line can be given a little exit flick.

Exit flicks will help you get from one letter to the next when you start to join letters.

Trace.

a d h i k l m n t u v w

Track these letters with exits.

a a a a a a a a a

d d d d d d d d d

h h h h h h h h h

i i i i i i i i i

k k k k k k k k k

l l l l l l l l l

m m m m m m m

Track these letters with exits.

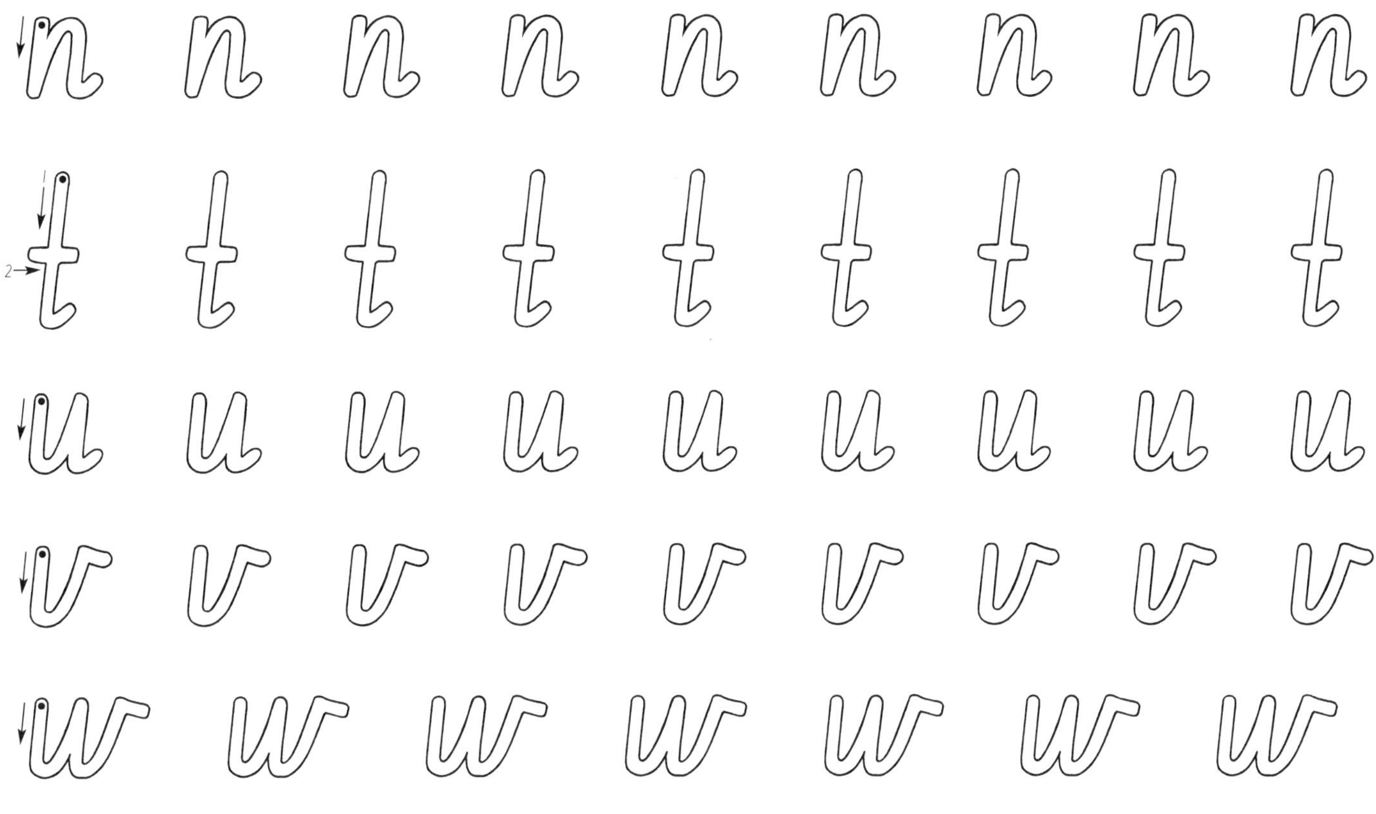

Trace these, then write your own.

a d h
i k l
m n t
u v w

Exits

Trace these letters with exits.

a a a a a a d d d d d

h h h h h h i i i i i i

k k k k k k l l l l l l

m m m m m n n n n n

t t t t t t u u u u u u

v v v v v v w w w w w

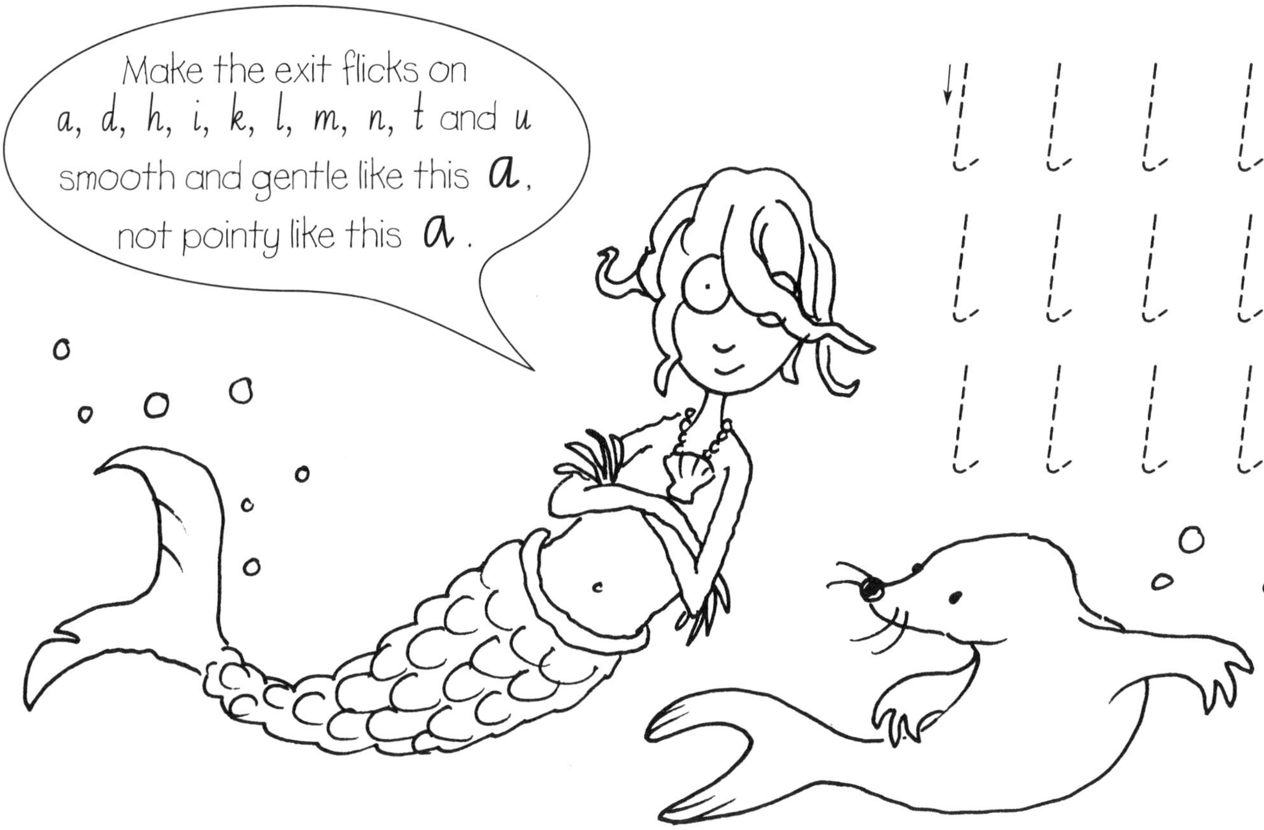
Make the exit flicks on a, d, h, i, k, l, m, n, t and u smooth and gentle like this a, not pointy like this a.

Here are some kinds of pirate treasures. Trace, then copy.

silver emeralds weapons gold

wine velvet spices silk rubies

pieces of eight sapphires

Self Assessment

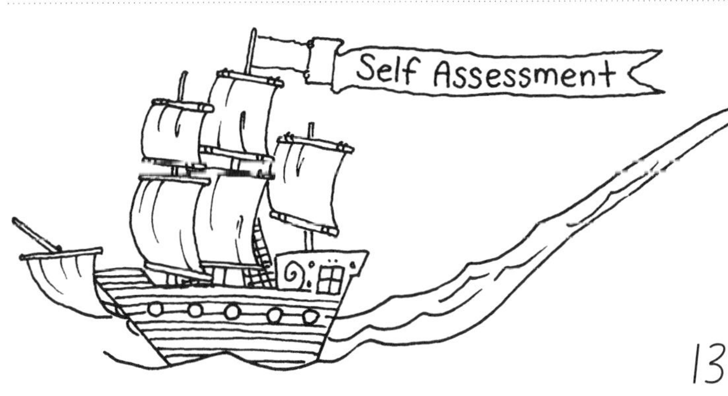

Tick the letters that have smooth exit flicks. Circle your best one.

Exits

top point

v

little dip

w

Rewrite the passage below. Add exit flicks to the letters that need them.

Pirates are thieves who sail the seas looking for vessels to steal from. They hold up the ship's crew using guns, knives and other weapons. They steal whatever treasures are on board.

Trace and copy the names of places pirates sailed to.

Indian Ocean Arabian Sea

Jamaica South China Sea

Cape of Good Hope Cuba

Straits of Malacca

The Spanish Main

Exits

Trace and copy.

Madagascar is an island in the

Indian Ocean. In the 1600s

and 1700s, it became known

as Pirate Island — so many

pirates lived there. They raided

ships that were going to India

laden with gold and silver.

Trace and copy.

The pirates raided the ships on

their way back to Europe, too.

But these ships usually carried

spices, silk, tea and coffee,

which were harder to sell.

Put a tick ✓ next to your best word.

Exits

Trace. Add exits to the letters that need them.

The food taken on long voyages had to be preserved by drying and salting. Fresh food would run out not long into the voyage. Sailors went ashore on islands to restock with fresh food and water.

List some foods the sailors might hope to find.

Assessment page – Exits

Trace, then do your own.

a a d d

h h i i

k k l l

m m n n

t t u u

Trace, then do your own.

v v w w

Rewrite the sentence. Add exit flicks to the letters that need them.

The minke whale leapt out of the water and waved its tail.

Teacher

Introducing entries

Trace.

i j m n p r u v w y

Track these letters with entries.

i i i i i i i i i

j j j j j j j j j

m m m m m m m

n n n n n n n n n

p p p p p p p p p

r r r r r r r r r

u u u u u u u u u

v v v v v v v v v

Track these letters with entry flicks.

w w w w w w w

y y y y y y y y y

Trace these letters with entry flicks. Then try your own.

i j

m n

p r

u v

w y

Trace. Add entry and exit flicks to the letters that need them.

a b c d e f g h i

j k l m n o p q r

s t u v w x y z

Entries

Trace.

Trace, then copy.

bow hull jib compass stern

prow galley crow's nest

cannon figurehead mainsail

yardarm sails rigging mast

Circle your best word. Tick ✓ your best entry flick.

Entries

Trace and copy.

Figureheads on sailing ships

were common in ancient

times. They were attached to

the prow of the ship. They

were often in the shape of

mermaids, dragons or lions.

Trace and copy.

Figureheads were often carved

from wood, then painted.

Some even had gold on them.

They were thought to bring

good luck or ward off evil.

Capitals and entries

Trace the titles of these books about mermaids. Add the entry flicks to the letters that need them.

Capital letters don't have entry flicks because they don't join up to other letters.

"The Little Mermaid" by Hans Christian Andersen

"The Merman" by Dick King-Smith

"Aquamarine" by Alice Hoffman

"Deep Trouble", Goosebumps No. 19 by R. L. Stine

"A Treasury of Mermaids: Mermaid Tales from Around the World" by Shirley Climo

Rewrite the information in the lines.
Add entry flicks to the letters that need them.

Francis Drake was an English sea captain. Queen Elizabeth I ordered him to attack Spanish ships. He brought her a lot of gold. She made him a knight in 1581.

Remember – some letters need an exit flick as well as an entry flick!

Self Assessment

How would you rate your entry flicks?

Entries

Trace then copy these pirate sayings.

Land ahoy! Aye, aye, Cap'n!

Splice the mainbrace!

Shiver me timbers!

Avast, me hearties!

Hoist the Jolly Roger!

Assessment page – Entries

Trace these letters with entry flicks, then do your own.

i i j j n n

m m p p

r r u u v v

w w y y

Write the letters that have an entry flick only, four times each.

Write the letters that have both an entry flick and an exit flick, two times each.

Teacher

Trace, then copy. Add entries to the letters that need them. Remember that some letters will need exits too.

Walk the plank, you scurvy dog!

Introducing diagonal joins

Trace and copy these letter pairs using diagonal joins.

ae ai aj am an ap ar au

ce ce ci ci cr cr cu cu cy cy

de di dp dr du du dy dy

ee ei ej em en ep er eu ev ew

Trace and copy these letter pairs with diagonal joins.

he he hi hi hu hu hy hy ie

im im in in ir ir ke ki kn

kr ku ky ky le le li li lm

lu ly ly me mi mm mn mp

my ne ni nn nr nu nv ny

Circle your three best pairs of joining letters.

Diagonal joins

Trace the patterns. Turn them into fish.

Trace these letter pairs with diagonal joins.

te te ti ti tm tn tp tr tu ty

ue ui um un un up ut ur uy

Most letters with diagonal joins meet at the top body line.

Put a dot to show the line where the letters meet.

Trace these words with diagonal joins.

sardine blenny anemone

stingray marlin tuna

Trace and copy. Cross out the nonsense word.

deep keep sleep steep

lip hip tune dune mune

Diagonal joins to head and body letters

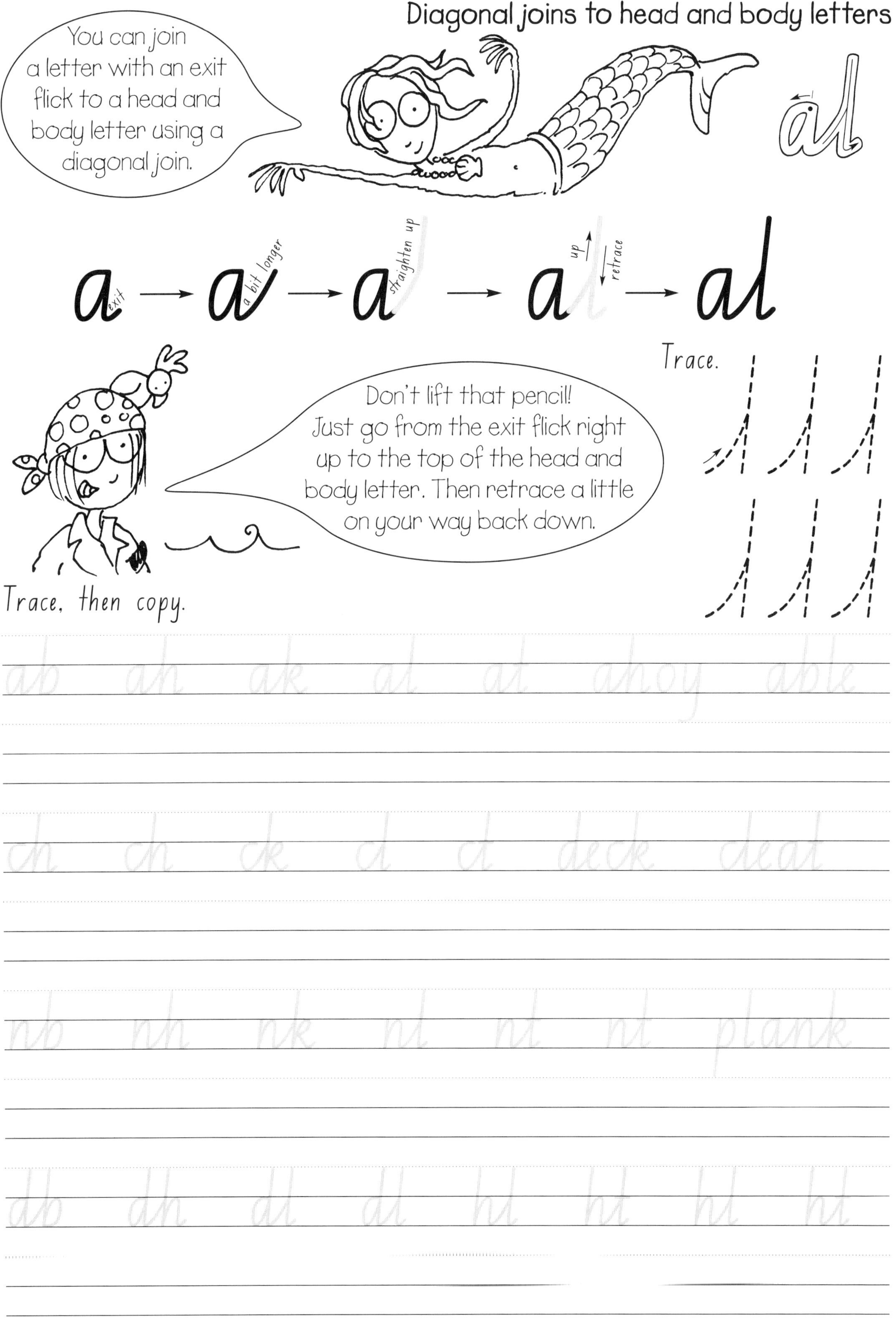

Diagonal joins to head and body letters

Trace and copy.

lb lb lk ll ll lt galley

th th tl tl tt tt cutlass

ub uh uk ul ut mutiny

kl kh kl kh mb ml mb

eb ek et keel ik il it jib

q q q q q q q q q q q

qu qu qu qu qu qu qu qu

Trace and copy.

quite quite quiet quill quit

z z

z z

z z z z z z z z z z z

ze zi zu zy zl zzzz zzzz

Trace and copy.

zip zeal lazy wheeze swizzle

Diagonal joins

Check list

- ☐ Posture
- ☐ Pencil grip
- ☐ Paper position

Write these words underneath in joined-up writing.

ant ate link mink

cup nun den met

kite belly smelly heel keel

hip tip limb numb quiz quit

quiet hill dew size sneeze

Assessment page – Diagonal joins

Show how these letter pairs look when they are joined.

ti up hy le mm ir kn

nu qu ev cy an dr ze er

Show how these letter pairs look when they are joined.

ch ck nk lk il zl at ll

nt th et ab it ub ut lt

Write these words in joined-up writing.

time kilt link mum new

hut they them quite zip

Introducing drop-in joins

Remember these anti-clockwise letters? Put a dot to show where each letter starts. Then put an arrow to show the direction you move in.

a c d g o q

These letters are dropped into place when you join them to a letter that has an exit flick.

Make the exit flick come up a bit higher, so it nearly reaches the top body line.

lift pencil at star

ud

lift pencil here

u → ud → ud

Trace.

ia ia ha ha ha ma ma

ma ac ac ac ec ec ec

uc uc ad ad ed ed ed

id id id eg eg eg lg lg

ag ag ag ug ug lo lo

lo no no no to to to

aq aq eq eq iq iq nq

Drop-in joins

Trace the dropped-in letter.
Copy the letter pair. Put a star ✳ at the place where the letters meet.

ca ua ma cc tc ic ad nd

dd ig dg ng do mo co aq

Trace and copy.

mad coo ice day zoo lid

tick tug dig aqua inquire

udder and edge money equal

The new f

Trace and copy.

af uf ef if if lf mf nf uf

Finish these letter pairs by adding f.

a m d e i l n u

Trace and copy.

fluff diff tiff cuff huff

sniff if deaf leaf life wife

Trace and copy.

Trace and copy. Change colour when you lift your pencil for a drop-in join.

Drop-in joins

Assessment page – Drop-in joins

Show what these letter pairs look like joined.

na ca ld aq ec ug eg mo

nd ea ic ig eq id cc ad

Write these words in cursive writing. Put a star ✳ at each place where you lifted your pencil.

aqua each handle accent

leg called halo equip udder

Write these words in cursive. Change colour when you lift your pencil for a drop-in join.

leaf half if whiff

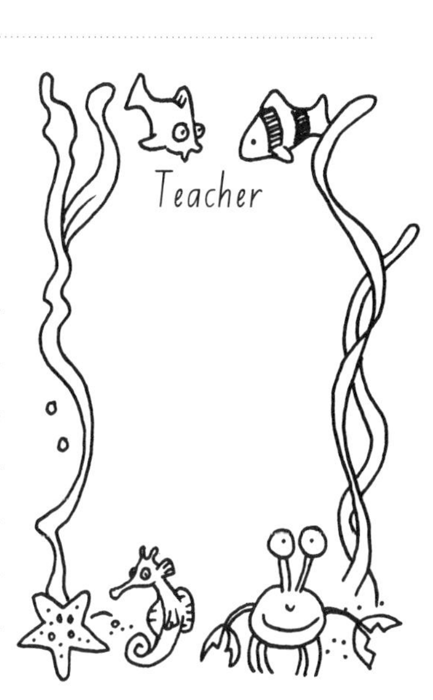

Introducing horizontal joins

The horizontal join from o, r, v, w and x has a little ______ .

Trace and copy.

rm rn rp rr ru rv rw

vy vi vy vu vy vu vv vi

vu vv wi wn wi wr wu

wn wr wu wm wr wm wr

xi xy xu xu xi xp xy

Horizontal joins to anti-clockwise letters

When you make a horizontal join to an anti-clockwise letter, go across to the start of the letter, then retrace along the top.

rc retrace wa od vo xa

Trace and copy.

oa coat oc lock og dog

od cod oo zoo oa oc od

ra race rc arc rd heard

rg urge ro rope rd rd rg

va vacancy vo voice va vo

Trace and copy.

wa wary wa wait wo word

xa exact xc excel xo exodus

xq exquisite xa xc xo xq

Trace and copy these underwater words.

waves shoal rockpool surgeonfish

ocean octopus valley frogfish

Self Assessment

Circle your three best horizontal joins to anti-clockwise letters.

Horizontal joins from f

Horizontal joins to head and body letters

Trace and copy.

ol ob oh ol of rl rk rt rb

wk wl wt wh xl xt xf xl xt

Trace and copy these words.

otter oblong hollow off where

surfboard work next when who

Horizontal joins

Trace and copy.

Check list

- [ ] Posture
- [ ] Pencil grip
- [ ] Paper position

goblin megamouth

white frilled porbeagle

hammerhead smoothhound lemon

whitetip wobbegong prickly

leopard dogfish zebra nurse

These are all names of sharks. Write your favourite one twice.

Assessment page – Horizontal joins

Write these words in cursive.

out river toxic hurry own

ring vital burn wish boil

Horizontal joins to anti-clockwise letters

railroad vacuum wave

coal urgent exact word

Horizontal joins from f

from family forward

Horizontal joins to head and body letters

whirl often sixty flan

Introducing letters that don't join

Put a cross **x** to show where the letter ends. Draw an arrow to show the direction your pencil is going in as you finish the letter.

b g j p s y

Trace.

be ga ju pr sl yo bl gi sn

Trace and copy the names of these corals. Change colour each time you lift your pencil.

brain staghorn gorgonian

slipper grape Juliet's lace

purple-polyped plankton-eater

bottlebrush finger table

Letters that don't join to e

fe oe re
ve we xe

Sea stars are echinoderms, like urchins and feather stars. They have five or more arms. Sea stars also have tube feet and a central feeding disc.

Tick the e's that aren't joined.
Circle your best word.

Letters that don't join – Capitals

Trace and copy these names. Then try some of your own.

April Angelfish Jessie Jellyfish

Odo Oyster Ignacio Isopod

Raju Rabbitfish Sybil Sweetlip

B L

C P

Write your own name. Circle the letters that don't join to the next letter.

Assessment page – Letters that don't join

Write these letter pairs in cursive writing.

ba ye jo pr gn se bl ph gr

Write these words in cursive. Then underline the letter pairs that don't join.

bear pear wear rear fear

axe have toe goal blend

spoke joke jelly elbow gypsy

Write these words in cursive. Circle the letter pairs that don't join.

Australia Fiji

Japan Indonesia

Look at this writing. Circle all the errors.

When h andwriting is even,
the words are often far
easier t o write and to read.

Use this check list to help you spot the errors.

Check for:			
even spacing	table	NOT	ta ble
careful retracing	aloof	NOT	aloof
small dips	wool	NOT	wool
the new f	fast	NOT	fast
drop-in joins	head	NOT	he a d
even slope	little	NOT	little

Rewrite the sentence correctly.

Rewrite the sentences correctly. Use the list on the previous page to help you.

Sirens are mythological
creatures.

They have the bodies of birds
and the heads of women.

They lured boats onto the
rocks with their sweet singing.

Consolidation – Practising joins

Copy each sentence. Then write T for true, or F for false.

The answers are at the bottom of page 59.

1. Giant squid eyes are as large as dinner plates.

2. Giant squid have the same number of legs as an octopus.

3. The only known predator of the giant squid is the sperm whale.

4. Giant squid are often seen swimming in the deep ocean.

5. The largest recorded giant squid was 18 metres long.

6. If attacked, a giant squid can squirt out a cloud of ink.

Answers: 1 T, 2 F, 3 T, 4 F, 5 T, 6 T

Self Assessment

Circle your best diagonal join from q to u. Underline your best word.

Before you start:

- circle the horizontal joins
- underline the diagonal joins to head and body letters
- put a star on the dropped-in letters to show where they touch the letter before.

Then copy these ocean facts.

Average ocean depth – 5000 m

Deepest part of ocean – 11 km

Earth covered by ocean – 2/3

Length of blue whale – 29 m

Smallest adult fish – goby (1cm)

Trace and copy.

In Greek mythology, Poseidon was the god of the sea. He had a long beard and held a trident (three-pronged spear).

Write an example of each kind of join. Find the examples in the text above.

a diagonal join ______

a drop in join ______

a horizontal join to a head and body letter ______

a diagonal join to a head and body letter ______

a horizontal join ______

a letter that doesn't join ______

Consolidation – Practising joins

Choose the items for the menu at my underwater café. Write them in cursive script. Write the price next to each item.

seaweed spaghetti	clam chowder	fish and chips
lobster bisque	krill salad	caviar on toast
prawn cocktail	barnacle pie	toffee brittlestar
jellyfish and custard	angelfish cake	coral crackers
plankton stew	sponge pudding	sea cucumber sandwiches

Entrée:

Main Course:

Dessert:

Remember to use printing when you label diagrams and maps.

Use these words to label the shark, using printing script:

pectoral fin	snout	gill slits	caudal fin	nostril
anal fin	dorsal fin	eye	mouth	pelvic fin

Now write the words in cursive script.

Consolidation – Practising joins

Imagine you are a creature that lives in the sea. Write a diary entry telling about a day in your life. Remember to write the date at the top.

Diary of a sea creature

Self Assessment

Check your work for

even spacing

careful retracing